MY
MASSACHUSETTS

My MASSACHUSETTS

By Elisabeth Villa

Illustrated by Nicole Fazio

Little
Beach
Books

Text copyright © Elisabeth Villa, 2013
Illustrations copyright © Nicole Fazio, 2013

All rights reserved, including the right of reproduction in whole or in part in any form.

ISBN: 978-0-9891340-0-2
Library of Congress Control Number: 2013935411

First Edition

All inquiries should be addressed to:

Little Beach Books
P.O. Box 6148
Falmouth, ME 04105

info@littlebeachbooks.com
www.littlebeachbooks.com
207.878.8804

Printed and manufactured by C&C offset Printing Co. Ltd. in China.
The illustrations in this book were executed in watercolor and acrylic ink on Arches paper.

The Freedom Trail® is a registered trademark. The use of the Freedom Trail® in this book is granted
with permission from the Freedom Trail Foundation.

Thank you to Boston Duck Tours, The Freedom Trail Foundation, The Naismith Memorial Basketball Hall of Fame,
The Swan Boats of Boston and the Witch House for granting permission to be included in this book.

For Alex,
Without you I never would have discovered
all there is to love about Massachusetts.

EV

For Dad,

Thank you for always lending a creative hand.

NF

My Massachusetts
is Paul Revere's ride—

time spent in the Bay State
will fill you with pride.

Beaches, lakes, forests
and great cities too...

explore with your friend
all the fun things to do!

Boston's the state's largest city of all.

Some buildings are old,
and some buildings are tall.

Sit on a duck,
take a slow Swan Boat ride,

pretend you're a sailor on "Old Ironsides."

A Freedom Trail walk gives us lessons firsthand
on winning our freedom from old England.

Paul Revere's ride got the Revolution humming—
by warning the colonists:

"The British are coming!"

From Sandwich to Provincetown there are beaches galore.
It's always a blast on Cape Cod's breezy shore.

Nantucket and Martha's Vineyard offer island escapes,
with whale watches, carousels and ferries from the Cape.

My Massachusetts is for watching a game,
and someday the crowd might be cheering *my* name.

Patriots, Celtics, the Sox...Bruins, too!
For sports fans in Mass., there's just so much to do.

Basketball started
in our own Bay State.

There's even a museum
to honor the greats.

Remember—when you play
or watch the NBA—

it began with a peach basket
right here in MA.

Gloucester's fine fishing fleet takes to the sea
to bring back fresh seafood for you and for me.

The South Shore is known for its cranberry crop.
They flood all the fields to get every last drop.

The Berkshires are mountains, though not very tall—
come peep at our leaves in the cool crisp of fall.

Salem's the place
for a Halloween parade.

It's all in good fun, though,
so don't be afraid!

My state's home to Plymouth, where Pilgrims did land.
So tired and hungry—they needed a hand.

More turkeys and pumpkins the natives kept bringing,
all to be shared at the first Thanksgiving.

So come *pahk* the *cah*—take a ride on the T!
You'll tour the big city or head to the sea.

History beckons, adventure awaits...

In my Massachusetts,
life truly is great.

To order books please visit our website,

www.LittleBeachBooks.com

or contact us by phone or email,

207. 878. 8804

orders@littlebeachbooks.com

My Massachusetts can also be ordered

through your local independent bookstore.